EGG
SOLID

An Introspective View On Success + A Step by Step Guide to Achieving Your Goals

By **JOHN THOMAS**

DISCLAIMER

The advice contained in this material might not be suitable for everyone. The author designed the information to present his opinion about the subject matter. The reader must carefully investigate all aspects of any business decision before committing to him or herself. The author obtained the information contained herein from sources he believes to be reliable and from his own experience, but he neither implies nor intends any guarantee of accuracy. The author is not in the business of giving legal, accounting, or any other type of professional advice. Should the reader need such advice, they must seek services from a competent professional. The author particularly disclaims any liability, loss, or risk taken by individuals who directly or indirectly act on the information contained herein. The author believes the advice presented here is sound. Still, readers cannot hold her responsible for either their actions or the risk taken by individuals who directly or indirectly act on the information contained herein.

Published by The 411 Brand Foundation
Printed in the United States
Copyright © 2021 by John Thomas
ISBN 978-0578385129

DEDICATION

This book is dedicated to my late mother Clara Sharon Smith who passed away in January 2021. She was my biggest supporter and always encouraged me to chase my dreams boldly. Growing up, whatever I chose to focus on, she always told me to envision the outcome and ask myself will the journey to attain the outcome be worth the time required to achieve it.

I am extremely grateful for the knowledge and love that my mother has shared with me during her time here on earth. Without her unwavering faith and love, pursuing a goal that doesn't exist would've seemed impossible. It was her belief in me that has given me the confidence to know that I can do all things through Christ that strengthens me. Now, its my responsibility to honor her legacy by passing along these steps to achieving success with as many young people across the world that have decided to dedicate their lives to Striving for Greatness!!

Thank you to each and every person that has lifted a finger to assist me with building this organization over these 30 years. 411 Brand is like my child. My 30-year old child, that can now take care of himself in the world. He's able to build relationships, inspire people as well as play an important role in helping to pour life and inspiration into a generation of the leaders that will help shape the world that we live in. I do not take that responsibility lightly and I'm honored that God chose me to guide this dream into reality.

DEDICATION REQUEST

Please pass a copy of this book to anyone you care about
who is in need of some inspiration and motivation

ACKNOWLEDGEMENTS

I am extremely grateful for the knowledge and love that my mother has shared with me during her time here on earth. Without her unwavering faith and love, pursuing a goal that doesn't exist would've seemed impossible. It was her belief in me that has given me the confidence to know that I can do all things through Christ that strengthens me. Now, its my responsibility to honor her legacy by passing along these steps to achieving success with as many young people across the world that have decided to dedicate their lives to Striving for Greatness!!

Thank you to each and every person that has lifted a finger to assist me with building this organization over these 30 years. 411 Brand is like my child. My 30 year old child, that can now take care of himself in the world. He's able to build relationships, inspire people as well as play an important role in helping to pour life and inspiration into a generation of the leaders that will help shape the world that we live in. I do not take that responsibility lightly and I'm honored that God chose me to guide this dream into reality.

CONTENTS

INTRODUCTION

The Egg Solid Theory is a metaphor that separates those that are committed to working really hard to achieve their success and those that are interested in trying to look successful while mining for short cuts in life.

You enter a space and see that there are two eggs lying on the counter across the room. Are you able to tell which egg was boiled and which egg was taken directly out of the carton, without holding or getting real close to the eggs?

The boiled egg represents someone that has worked really hard to achieve their goals. The boiled egg has been placed on a stove and has been under fire for 12-15 minutes in order to become solid. The fire represents going through life's ups and downs. Not everything will go your way in life. When you're trying to get to the next level, you will hear the word no more times than you hear the word yes. You will have a few cracks, some bruises, but if you're really focused on achieving your goals, especially the ones that are aligned with your passion, then you must keep going.

Here is an example of going through the fire.

You may have an idea that you want to share with the world. You really believe in this idea but find out that your friends doesn't support your vision. Do you quit? No, you keep going! That is an example of going through the fire.

You're in the gym practicing on your game everyday. At the end of the game, when it's crunch time, your coach calls on you to take the last shot and you miss the game winner. You hear the gasp from the crowd, they're disappointed, your teammates are disappointed and you feel like you let everyone down. That is an example of going through the fire.

You're working hard to achieve your goals but along the journey you will have multiple setbacks. This is an example of going through the fire.

These are the types of situations that build character and a strong resilience to anything that may come in your path. When you're going through the fire, you build a tolerance to be able to withstand failure and use it as a learning lesson. Just like the egg that's been under fire for 15 minutes, you may have some exterior cracks that everyone can see but your foundation is solid. You're able to move through life more confidently because you've been through some things that allows you to make better choices in life.

The other egg that was pulled directly out of the carton symbolizes someone that looks for shortcuts in order to achieve his or her goals. They haven't been through much and expect handouts in life. If they try something and it doesn't work, they give up and quit. They complain that nobody supports or helps them to achieve their goals. When the game is on the line and the coach calls on them to take the last shot, they're not prepared. Instead of working on their game during the week, they are hanging out at parties with friends, spending time on social media instead of practicing on their game. So when the coach calls on them, they look confident, they look ready to take the shot. But when the coach draws up a play they miss the badly. The team is disappointed, the crowd is unhappy and the player that missed the shot, blames his teammates for not doing their job like setting a proper screen. This type of person will make excuses and give reasons why it's not their fault that they missed the shot. This is someone that isn't willing to go through the fire and take ownership for his or her actions. They know that they weren't practicing on their game. They weren't prepared for the opportunity. So the analogy between the boiled egg and the one directly out of the carton is this:

So many people want to look successful without going through the fire. They want to look like their favorite entertainer, athlete or CEO but are not willing to dedicate the many years to learning the craft without any accolades. The egg that has been through the fire, when it falls to the ground will only have a couple cracks and some dents on the outside but will still be solid on the inside. When the other egg that hasn't been through the fire falls to the ground, it will crack completely open and would have to be discarded and thrown away because the inside isn't solid. It hasn't been through the fire, which symbolizes going through some things in life that were challenging. There will always be peaks and valleys along the journey but you never give up. If you fall down seven times, you get up eight. Each time you get up, you're stronger, wiser and you become a valuable asset and resource to others striving for success as well.

My inspiration for writing this book is my oldest son Joshua. His mother and I separated and divorced when he was around 12 years old. It was a very difficult time because up until that point, Joshua was my shadow. Wherever I went he was there with me. Whether it was my job, AAU games, Hawks games, industry events, it didn't matter he was with me. So to now be going through this divorce, it was extremely challenging to not be in his life every single day.

Being able to live in the same home as your child is incredibly important to their childhood development. As a boy, he gets to watch his father's mannerisms, listen to his thoughts, receive advice and to be able to see firsthand how his father reacts to life's issues as man in this world. Also, as a father, being a part of your child's daily decisions and to immediately be able to share some of the wisdom and life lessons that I learned over the years with him in real time, was priceless.

As Joshua moved into his teenage years, his mother moved out of state and Joshua agreed to move with her for a fresh start. After a few months, he began making choices and decisions that weren't the greatest and not being there to confront those decisions in real time was a tough pill to swallow as a father or any parent in that situation. During our conversations, I would share my thoughts with him on various issues that he was facing but not being there to help him navigate through different situations in real time was tough. I began to feel the guilt slowly to creep into my life. Being unable to step in and make tough times easier was a learning lesson for me.

I've been blessed to work in the youth development industry for 30+ years. I naturally became a father figure to many of the kids I came in contact with over the years. The same advice I share with my children, I find myself sharing with other teenagers looking for success in their lives. So, I decided to share some of the principals I've learned over the years in this book.

I believe all kids have a desire to become successful in life. But how? First, we must define what success means to us. What is success? Is it money? Is it cars & homes? Is it love? Is it peace? What is it? Once you define what success means to you, then you must design a blueprint for you to follow in order to achieve your success. I will layout eight (8) steps that will help you create a strong foundation for success in your life.

I truly believe that if you can master each of these steps, you will find your success. Again, success is different for everyone. You determine your success from the inside out and not outside in. Society will have you thinking that money, cars, houses and other materialistic things are success. When I have all of that, it will mean that I'm successful. Those things are by-products of success. Success is personal and although others will have no problem telling you if you're successful or not, it would always be your choice to believe them.

These steps will focus on and help develop your foundation to either personal, social, academic, and athletic development. My approach to Character Education is structured around specific key concepts. These concepts provide a "moral compass" to guiding our attitudes and behaviors as well as to be able to clearly identify all of our personal, academic and athletic goals.

I will share personal examples, photos and never before heard stories of when I had to use each of these steps along my 30-year journey as the CEO/Founder of The 411 Brand Inc. Also, in an effort to show that these steps are universal, I reached out to a few friends, some I've known for over 40 years, and asked them to share how these steps have played a vital role in helping them achieve success in their lives.

Here are my Eight Steps to Success.....

FOCUS

1.

Focus
Focus *pl.* fo·cus a center of interest or activity.

Before you begin your pursuit of any goal, there should be laser focus on your WHY! You need to ask yourself, why am I doing this and what is the desired outcome. To focus, you must first eliminate any unnecessary noise in your life, especially if it's not helping you achieve your goal. Some examples are: Friends, Family Members, Social Media and Cell Phones. You have to have an unwavering dedication to achieving your goals. You will be challenged, pushed and tested. Accepted it, that's how you grow to the next level. Nothing should take you away from your goals especially if it's in alignment with your soul & spirit.

One day I reached out to my friend Chris Hicks, whom I have known for 25+ years to ask him how focused he was growing up, while trying to navigate his path to achieve the goals he set for himself. His reply was, "Growing up, I don't think that really I got in touch with what focus actually meant, as well as how to attribute it to my life journey and the importance of it. I lacked *having singular focus, blocking out all of the noise, blocking out all of the distractions, and really kind of harvesting every ounce of focus needed to get to where I wanted to go. So I don't think I was very focused at all." But if you know Chris, he definitely figured it out. Chris has had an incredible career in the music industry. He is one of the founders of the highly successful Noontime Music, home to over 35 No. 1 Billboard Hits. He has worked with and helped steer the careers of Mary J Blige, Usher, Aaliyah, Justin Bieber, just to name a few. Chris has taken his talents to the film industry and is currently the Chief Innovation Officer at Quality Control Holdings.*

For me, back in 1992, I was invited to the NBA Summer League Free Agent Camp in Los Angeles. As the week long camp was coming to a close, I realized that my aspiration and passion for playing in the NBA went out the door. I had a few opportunities to go overseas to play but my goal was to play in the NBA and if that didn't happen, I was comfortable moving on to the next phase of my life. As I went back to the room, I was immediately faced with the question, "What are you going to do now?"

I had my Bachelor's degree in Mass Communications & Journalism from Samford University, but I had not taken any steps or made any preparations to really use my degree immediately after graduation. Again, I thought my talents would get me to the league and then once I played a few years, I would begin to focus and plan on life after basketball. But that was not the case. I immediately had to figure out my next move and I needed to do it quick. I was out in Los Angeles with no money, no job and no prospects because my focus was totally on basketball.

So, while packing my things to fly back to my mother's house in Buffalo, New York, I started watching a television show where young people discussed a variety of issues going on in their lives. The host was an older gentleman, slightly out of touch but was able to get the students to open up and share their thoughts. It was at that moment when I realized that this is what I want to do in the next chapter of my life. I will create a program for young people that will bridge the gap between successful people and young people striving for success. I will create a talk show and invite celebrities to share their journey with young people with the hopes of assisting them with their goals of achieving success in their lives.

When I landed in Buffalo, I excitedly shared my idea with my parents. I didn't have any leads or potential opportunities waiting for me, it was just something inside me that told me that this was my path. My father, who was the Vice President of the Urban League in Buffalo told me that my first step should be writing down my idea in detail in a presentation format. It should be written in a way that lays out the idea so that whomever reads it, will understand the concept. How do you do that for a television concept? This information wasn't readily available, especially if you didn't know anyone in that field. During this time, Google didn't exist. I did as much research as possible to be sure that my vision was clear. I saw the vision vividly and although no one could see it like I could, it became my mission to see it all the way through.

I told my parents that I felt that the idea really wouldn't work in Buffalo. I told them that the few times I went to Atlanta, I really liked it and was thinking about moving there to jump-start the next phase of my life. We had a lot of family in Atlanta and they suggested that I call my cousin Carol Blackmon, who was a radio personality on V103 Radio. Carol was in the entertainment business and would really have her finger on the pulse of the city. She could really let me know if my idea would work in Atlanta and if so, possibly give me some advice on where to begin. I shared my vision with her in detail and really expressed my "WHY"! To my surprise, she got it. She explained the landscape there and really gave me the confidence to go for it 100%

When I arrived in Atlanta, with my best friend Andre' Colbert, we moved in with my late cousin Joyce Hilliard. She allowed us to move into her house until we got our thing together.

I talked to anyone that would listen to me about creating a place where we could close the gap between successful individuals and young people striving for success. I wanted to do it in a way that was entertaining, yet educational. The Oprah

Winfrey Show was huge during this time. I wanted to create an Oprah type show for young people. A program that had a strong positive impact but was specifically directed towards young people. I worked various odd jobs to be able to eat but my focus was turning this vision into reality. I surrounded myself with like-minded people as well as people that knew more than I did especially in the entertainment space.

Devoting my complete focus to achieving this goal was challenging, yet easy to me. I've always had the ability to lock in on things that really mattered. Being able to block out the noise and keeping the main thing...the main thing is key. There will be times when we're distracted and get off track, but if we have a goal that was born in our soul, which requires an intense focus in order to achieve, we will find our path back to striving for greatness.

To help you with strengthening your Focus

- Establish daily quiet time away from everything
- Spend time daily without social media
- Start to evaluate the relationships around you

Notes_____

_____

_____

_____

_____

_____

_____

_____

_____

_____

_____

_____

_____

_____

_____

_____

_____

_____

Notes_____

_____

_____

_____

_____

_____

_____

_____

_____

_____

_____

_____

_____

_____

_____

_____

_____

PASSION

2.

Passion
Passion n. pas·sion the object of such enthusiasm.

Your passion about something is equivalent to your love for it. When you have an unconditional love for something, no matter what happens along the way, you're not leaving it. One way to find out if you're passionate about a task, ask yourself, if I had to do this for 8-10 hours a day and not get paid for it, would I continue to do it? If the answer is yes, that's Passion!

One day, I was having a conversation with my friend Leslie "Big Lez" Segar to get her thoughts on the word Passion and how she was able to figure out what her passion was. She said, "Waking up before others, doing what burns in your soul, feeling the need to physically and artistically express yourself without praise or monetary motivation, is nothing but pure passion. A passion that for most of us, is our oxygen. It's definitely my oxygen!"

If you know Big Lez, then you understand that she is one of Hip Hop's Treasures! She's a multi-talented, highly respected dancer/choreographer along with an on-air radio & television personality/producer, that has tapped into her passion and built an incredible career along the way. In addition to dancing and providing choreography for the likes of LL Cool J, Mary J Blige, Michael Jackson, Whitney Houston and many more, she was a fixture on our television sets as a host and producer BET's Rap City.

When I first started 411, there was no monetary value to the program. I only had a concept on paper and a vision that I felt would inspire young people to maximize their full potential in this world. I had an idea of what I wanted to do but there weren't any examples available to me on where to begin. So, through reading several marketing books and biographies on people that inspired me (there was no internet at this time), I learned this method that is still extremely helpful to this day. I clear all of my thoughts and envision my perfect outcome to the task at hand. What it looks like, what it smells like, who was there, how I felt at that moment and then begin to work backwards to my current space. This requires a tremendous amount of focus and passion because its like you're moving around in the dark. You come across so many reasons to give up and settle for the easy route but deep down you realize that you will not reach your full potential by settling for anything less than the vision.

If you speak to anyone that has achieved any amount of success, they would be the first to tell you that they didn't do it alone. You have to be able to articulate your vision to others in such a clear way that they become excited about the vision as well. This will be your passion coming across helping them see the vision and get them interested in sharing their time and resources to assist with your vision. There's an old saying that if you're the smartest person in the room, you are in the wrong room.

One day through sheer frustration, I picked up the phone book (yes, the thick phone book) and looked up Coca-Cola. I knew the headquarters was in Atlanta and to me, it only made sense that they will be able to see the vision and the value of 411. Sprite was one of the leading brands targeting young people at the time and the potential impact this program could have with young people across the country should be enticing to the brand. So, I picked up the phone and cold called Coca-Cola. I didn't have a name, a department, a lead, a reference or anything.

"Hello ma'am, my name is John Thomas and I produce a program called the 411 Knowledge & Entertainment Show in Atlanta that bridges the gap between successful individuals and young people that are striving for success. We invite successful people on the show to share their journey to success to help give young people hope that they can achieve their hopes and dreams as well." Over the past two years our guests have included Usher, OutKast, LL Cool J, Notorious B.I.G., Monica and many more. I would like to speak with someone at Sprite to see if there would be interested in sponsoring 411 for a Ten (10) City Summer Tour across the country?"

At this moment, I felt good that I didn't stumble and got everything off that I wanted to say but was it enough? Is this how you pitch ideas to Fortune 500 companies? The receptionist replied "I'll transfer you to someone at Sprite." Man, I felt defeated only because I just poured my heart out to the phone operator at Coca-Cola and her job is to manage calls for an entire company, SMH. A woman picked up the phone immediately and said, "Hello, how can I help you?" I snapped out of it and went back into my pitch. This time there was a little more conviction in my tone. After I finished she said, "well I am the receptionist for the Brand Managers here at Sprite and this sounds amazing. If you have anything in writing, please send it over asap and I would put in on the desk of one of Sprite's Brand Manager's that I think would be interested."

Now I'm caught between excited and nervous because what am I sending them? What does it need to include, how detailed etc. So, I asked her, "Do you want me to send over a description of the concept?" She said, "yes along with a complete budget of what it would cost for the tour, potential guests and everything needed to paint the picture for the Brand Manager." I replied, "Sounds great," as if I had it all together. I never put together a full budget before nor have I presented my vision to anyone in this position. I took the next couple of days to put together the best presentation packet I could (it was only 5 sheets lol) and sent it over. To my surprise, I received a call from the receptionist asking if I was able to come to Coca-Cola for a meeting with the Brand Manager next week. Wow! This is moving too fast! Am I ready? What do I say? What do I wear? Remember, just 4 days ago, I was stressed out not knowing what I was going to do with 411 to now being invited to sit in front of Sprite's Brand Manager to ask for support for my vision. After sharing the vision, as well as my past and what led me up to the moment, the Brand Manager stood up and said, "John, I'm excited about this opportunity! The passion you shared for this project really has me looking forward to the possibilities and impact, we could have with 411!" As I stood up, my jaw dropped (not literally, gotta play it cool) as I shook his hand. He said, "I look forward to working with you."

Although I am not an overly dramatic person, I was able to share my passion for 411 in a way to get someone else excited to financially support my vision. I know this is a very rare occurrence, but I always believe that what is for you, is for you. Stay ready so that you do not have to get ready.

One of the great things that Lez shared with me about her story that was similar to mine was her desire to find a way when there seemed not to be one. "I thank God my Mother decided to water this tree and put me into a YMCA," Lez said. "Needless to say…she is shocked to this day, that it got me a full scholarship to college and later allowed me to visit 5 of 7 continents around the world dancing with the biggest celebrities on the planet."

To help you find your Passion

- Ask yourself, what would you do for free?
- What are you so good at that people would pay you to do it?
- What do you enjoy doing that makes you happy?

Notes_____

_____

_____

_____

_____

_____

_____

_____

_____

_____

_____

_____

_____

_____

_____

_____

Notes_____

_____

_____

_____

_____

_____

_____

_____

_____

_____

_____

_____

_____

_____

_____

_____

_____

_____

_____

PRACTICE

3.

Practice
Practice v. prac·tice to do or perform (something) repeatedly, in order to polish a skill.

No matter how much talent you have, in order to become GREAT, you must practice your craft over and over again. Repetition creates habits and if you're constantly repeating steps to make you better, eventually you will become GREAT at it. This rule works both ways though. If you consistently practice bad habits, it's those bad habits that you will become GREAT at. When I got my first opportunity to share my vision, I took it and ran with it. I treated the opportunity as if it was the gateway to achieving my goal.

I reached out to my guy Javin Foreman, a good friend that has really helped with the growth and development of the 411 Brand. I asked him his thoughts on the word Practice and what did the word mean to him? He said,"The word practice to me means being in the lab! This is that time in your life when you to take an active role in figuring out who you are. Its a time to work on your craft before you really go out and show the world your gift. Practicing helps you become confident in who you are and what you have to offer the world. Its important that you use your time and use your imagination to figure out who you are as well as how to utilize the gifts that you have been blessed with."

Javin has worked in youth development for 20+ years and helped thousands of young people develop a successful strategic plan for their lives in Chicago. Currently, in Atlanta he continues to impact young people through basketball along with owning a Marketing and Visual Communications company. With two sons and a daughter of his own, Javin says that he shares with them a famous quote from Muhammad Ali when asked about practicing. He said that "Champions are made when nobody is looking. Champions are made in the rain, in the gym, when nobody is around."

While working at V103 Radio as a Promotions Coordinator, one of my many responsibilities (if you worked in radio, you know that you essentially have 10 jobs) was managing all of the prizes that were given away over the radio. One day, Carol Blackmon, one of the Morning Show Personalities, came to my desk to ask if she could have some prizes to give to students at a Career Day she was invited to speak at in East Point. I asked her, "What exactly did she have to do at the school." As she explained, my mind went directly to this could be our chance to begin bringing 411 to life. I asked her, "Instead of having a normal career day conversation, what do you think about me executing the 411 concept I shared with you before moving to Atlanta with you being the host?" Carol thought it was a good idea and suggested that I call the school to pitch my idea to see what they would say. I called the following day and spoke with Ms. Denise Washington in the Arts Department. We had a great conversation, and the school was 100% on board. Now, I have my first opportunity to bring my vision to life.

As I mentioned earlier, I had a full vision of the outcome and began to work backwards. What do I need, what should we talk about, who would be the guest, what would the set look like and hundreds of more questions soon followed. I was excited to really have this opportunity and put everything I had into it.

The show went extremely well. The topic that we discussed was, "What goes into being a successful recording artist?" We invited Brad Davidson who worked in A&R at Jive Records to share his journey, along with what actually goes into making a successful record and getting it played on the radio. The students asked a lot of questions and everyone involved looked at the program as a huge success.

The next day, I sat down with Ms. Washington to discuss the outcomes of the program. She really liked the show and felt that the students were engaged from start to finish. I asked about the possibility of returning and she said of course, we are welcomed whenever we like to return. So, we decided to adopt the school and produce a show each month at the school and discuss various topics that affect young people. We invited different celebrity guests each month to share their journey with the students.

With this incredible opportunity, there was instantly a lot of responsibility that followed. I had to manage securing all of the guests for each show, writing the scripts, deal with the school administration, students, hosts, equipment etc. But this was our opportunity to Practice everyday to perfect our craft.

For 7 years, we didn't receive a dime. We had a guest list on the show over those years that rivaled any national television program. Guests included Notorious B.I.G., Usher, OutKast, Goodie Mob, Jermaine Dupri, Da Brat, LL Cool J and many more. We looked like we were getting financial support because of the professionalism, consistency, access and the full support from friends that really believed in the vision. Yes, I had to come out of pocket for a lot of things, but I looked at it as an investment into the bigger prize. I was given an opportunity to really perfect the vision while actually figuring out our next move.

In order to create value, you must create something that would be valuable to other people. There is no timetable on when someone would support your vision. So in the meantime continue to practice perfecting your craft and stay ready for when that opportunity presents itself to you.

To help with learning how to practice

- Research & Study the person doing what you want to do in detail.

- Find a way to do what you love to do as much as you can.

- Be still, visualize the journey & make sure what you're doing in real life matches the vision

Notes_____

_____

_____

_____

_____

_____

_____

_____

_____

_____

_____

_____

_____

_____

_____

_____

_____

Notes_____

_____

_____

_____

_____

_____

_____

_____

_____

_____

_____

_____

_____

_____

_____

_____

CONFIDENCE

4.

Confidence n. con·fi·dence
A feeling of assurance, especially of self-assurance.

O nce you master a certain skill you instantly become confident in your ability to carry out that skill. As a baby, you
don't start out knowing how to walk. You crawl until you can
take a step. After the first step, you fall down, get back up and
continue to keep taking a step. After putting together a series of
steps in between falls, you become confident in your ability to
walk. Soon, you're not even thinking about your steps, you're so
confident in your ability, that walking becomes second nature
to you. To get from one room to another do you think about
walking or do you just walk?

I reached out to my friend Tamera "Ty" Young and asked was
there ever a point in her life where she had to lean on her
self-confidence in order to achieve one of her goals. She said,
"When I was in high school preparing for college, I was unsure
of what school I should attend. Being an athlete, I knew I
wanted to go to a school where I could make a difference, as

well as make it to the WNBA. The route I chose wasn't the most common route. It took confidence to believe in my ability that no matter what school I chose, my dreams could come true." Ty chose to attend James Madison University in Virginia. She had a stellar college career and went on to become the 8th Pick of the 2008 WNBA Draft for the Atlanta Dream. She said, "God directed my path of course, however, with the help of my family and close friends believing and encouraging me along with the confidence I had in myself, really helped my dream become reality."

In the early stages of making my dream into a reality, I began to look for opportunities to grow the program with the more confidence that we were gaining. I started receiving calls from major record labels asking for our schedule so that they could get their artist on the show. We began getting articles written about the show in the Atlanta Journal & Constitution, as well as having the local news stations come out to see what we were doing. Honestly, we were feeling ourselves lol. There was no budget, just well-maintained relationships, vision and support. I felt that sky was the limit for the program.

I met with one of my good friends, Celeste Moses to share my frustrations of trying to grow to the next level. She really supported 411 and the way she spoke about the show to others always made me feel confident in what we were doing. I went to her a lot to bounce off the ideas I had in regards to the show. You have to understand, the 411 Brand didn't exist. It was being created in real time. Honestly, looking back I really have to give myself some credit for having the courage to live my dreams. Everything that happened with 411 came from a vision of what I thought the next steps were for 411. But in that, there were some insecurities that I had to navigate. Creating a narrative inside of my mind that I had to have all the answers, brought on unnecessary stress at times.

One day, Celeste and I were talking. I shared with her my vision to take the show outside of the school system, so that we would not be restricted with the topics that we could discuss, as well as the type of guests that we wanted to invite. But, without a budget or sponsor, how can we afford our own space? With the schools, we already had a built-in audience. If we moved outside of the school system, we would need to find a way to consistently attract young people to attend the program. Celeste mentioned that she was good friends with the Hip Hop legend MC Lyte, who recently moved to Atlanta. She thought that by introducing us, it could spark some inspiration in me as I tried to figure out the next move. Again, this is MC Lyte! She's one of my favorite MC's and I have been given this opportunity to not only meet her, but become vulnerable and admit that I needed some help with growing 411.

A couple of weeks later, Celeste called me and said that she spoke with Lyte and that she is looking forward to meeting with me and help out however she can. Celeste sent me the address and the following day I was driving to meet MC Lyte. I pulled up to this nice house and immediately got nervous. What do I say? What am I specifically asking for? What if she say I can't help you? All sorts of things were going through my head as I walked to the door. I rang the doorbell and an attractive woman answered the door smiling and said, "Hello, how can I help you?" I know MC Lyte's real name is Lana but I felt like I didn't know her well enough to call her by her government name but also calling someone by their rap name seemed weird to me. As I was about to say her name, Lyte appeared at the top of the stairs and said, "John?" A feeling came over me that I really couldn't describe. She said my name as if we were long lost friends, yet I've never met her before. How professional do I need to be in addressing her? Before I could think, I said, "What up Lyte, how are you?"

As she was walking down the stairs she smiled and said, "Come in, its great to meet you. I've heard great things about you and 411!" I immediately felt a sense of relief and started to become very comfortable in the situation. I shared with her my vision for the program and what we were able to do without much support from any sponsors over the years. She seemed genuinely interested in our journey and started brainstorming about how she could assist in anyway. She mentioned that she was great friends with a woman name Taylor Michaels, who was the Vice President of Magic Johnson Theaters. Magic

Johnson built an incredible movie theater in the Greenbriar section of Atlanta to help bring quality entertainment and restaurants to underserved communities across the country. Lyte suggested that possibly having a conversation with Taylor could open the door for 411 to make its home inside the theater. Lyte called Taylor at that moment, pitch the idea and Taylor agreed to speak with me the following day.

When I met with Taylor, I shared our journey with 411 and my vision for the program moving forward. I asked if we could produce our program inside the large movie theater once a month and invite schools to bring students to the program as a field trip. I really wanted a place of our own outside of the schools because I felt that we were starting to water down the program because of the limitations inside of the schools. We had to really be careful and only discuss topics and invite guests that are approved by the school. It was hard to censure some of the guests especially the new guys that were just coming up. I remember when we invited OutKast to be a guest on 411 at Southwest Dekalb High School (where Andre 3000 went to High School). At the end of the program, OutKast was asked to do an impromptu freestyle. I thought this would be dope but at the same time, these guys were free spirits. They dropped a few inappropriate words that had me staring at the principal hoping he didn't hear it or didn't understand it lol. But with the students reaction to the freestyle, I quickly realized that the show was a hit and that this was an incredible moment in our journey.

This partnership with Magic Johnson Theaters would give us an opportunity to bring more than one school at a time to each show. This will also begin to expand the program throughout Atlanta. Taylor thought it was a great idea and agreed on the spot. With Magic Johnson Theaters being new to the community, she saw 411 as a way to reach the parents of those kids in our program to bring their entire family to the theater.

Taylor connected me with the managers of the theater and they were great. There gave us unlimited access to the theater and really made us feel at home. My confidence at this point was on another level because I'm actually doing what I set out to do. It was really happening. There was so much more to do but I was excited to do it. Its an incredible feeling to wake up and live inside of your dreams.

To help with establishing your confidence

- Be really good at what you say you're good at
- Understand the difference between confidence and arrogance
- Never give up on it especially if you're passionate about it

Notes

Notes

_____

_____

_____

_____

_____

_____

_____

_____

_____

_____

_____

_____

_____

_____

_____

_____

_____

_____

_____

_____

_____

John Thomas & Da Brat at The 411 Knowledge & Entertainment Show at Underground Atlanta 1994

Da Brat & DJ Jelly at The 411 Knowledge & Entertainment Show at Underground Atlanta 1994

Big Boi, Carol Blackmon, Andre' 3000, Mr DJ and John Thomas at Southwest Dekalb High School 1994

Kenny Burns of The 411 Session at Clark Atlanta University 2012

CeeLo Green on The 411 Knowledge & Entertainment Show at Tri-Cities High School in East Point in 1994

Shanti Das of The 411 Session at Clark Atlanta University 2012

Kenny Burns of The 411 Session at Clark Atlanta University 2012

Jive Records Brad Davidson on The 411 Knowledge & Entertainment Show at Woodland Middle School 1993

Students on The 411 Knowledge & Entertainment Show at Southwest Dekalb High School 1994

Students on The 411 Knowledge & Entertainment Show at Columbia High School 1993

Jive Records Brad Davidson and Carol Blackmon on The 411 Knowledge & Entertainment
Show at Woodland Middle School 1993

Ryan Cameron and Immature on The 411 Knowledge & Entertainment Show at Woodland Middle School 1995

Ryan Cameron on The 411 Knowledge & Entertainment Show at Woodland Middle School 1995

47

Usher at The 411 Knowledge & Entertainment Show at the Roxy Theater 1995

Jennifer Walker and LL Cool J at The 411 Knowledge & Entertainment Show in 1995

John Thomas and Mista on The 411 Knowledge & Entertainment Show at the Olympic Superstore 1996

Jennifer Walker, John Thomas and Immature at The 411 Knowledge & Entertainment Show
at Woodland Middle School 1995

Packed house on the set of The 411 Knowledge & Entertainment Show at Woodland Middle School 1995

Chaka Zulu discussing HIV Education on The 411 Knowledge & Entertainment Show at the Olympic Superstore in 1996

The set of The 411 Knowledge & Entertainment Show at Woodland Middle School 1994

John Thomas, Chaka Zulu, DJ Jelly & Mista on the set of The 411 Knowledge & Entertainment Show at the Olympic Superstore 1996

The set of The 411 Knowledge & Entertainment Show at Woodland Middle School 1995

Ryan Cameron & John Thomas on the set of The 411 Knowledge & Entertainment
Show in 1994

Jennifer Walker and Monica 411 Interview at the Roxy Theater in 1995

Celeste Moses, Milo Calvacante' and Jennifer Walker on the set of The 411 Knowledge & Entertainment Show at Woodland Middle School in. 1995

John Thomas, Shanti Das and Teyon McCoy at the Hot 97.5 Community Awards Cere-mony in 1997

Kenny Burns on the set of The 411 Knowledge & Entertainment Show at Underground Atlanta 1995

John Thomas & Kenny Burns on the set of The 411 Knowledge & Entertainment Show at Underground Atlanta 1995

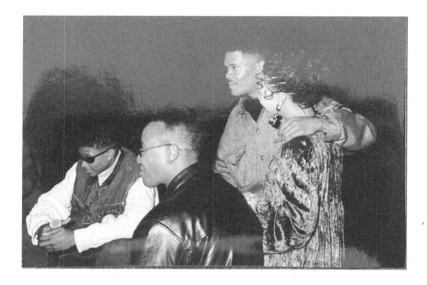

Usher, Ryan Cameron, Carol Blackmon and John Thomas on the set of The 411 Knowledge & Entertainment Show at Tri-Cities High School 1994

Carol Blackmon, Jonathon Slocumb & Lamont Boles on The 411 Knowledge & Entertainment Show at My Brother's Keeper in 1994

Students at The 411 Knowledge & Entertainment Show Sprite Tour in Atlanta in 1999

Carol Blackmon on the set of the 411 Knowledge & Entertainment Show at Underground Atlanta in 1994

John Thomas on the set of the Pilot Episode of The 411 Knowledge & Entertainment Show in 2000

Vernon Slaughter on the set of the 411/BMG Music Seminar at Magic Johnson Theaters in 1998

John Thomas with a member of the R&B Group BlackGirl and her mother on the set of The 411 Knowledge & Entertainment Show at Underground Atlanta in 1995

Kym Moye and R&B Singer Monica's brother on the set of The 411 Knowledge & Entertainment Show at The Roxy in 1995

John Thomas and Nick Grant at the 411 Brand Music Academy at Patchwerk Studios in 2018

John Thomas and Chaka Zulu in 2018

Students at the 411 Brand Basketball Academy POD in Midtown Atlanta in 2020.

Students at the 411 Brand Basketball Academy POD in Midtown Atlanta in 2020.

Students at the 411 Brand Lacrosse Academy in Midtown Atlanta in 2016

Students at the 411 Brand Basketball Academy POD in Midtown Atlanta in 2020.

Students at the 411 Brand Dance Academy in 2018

Students at the 411 Brand Soccer Academy in Midtown Atlanta in 2015

Students at the 411 Brand Music Academy at Patchwerk Studios in 2017

Students at the 411 Brand Music & Film Academy at Patchwerk Studios in 2017

Students at the 411 Brand Basketball Academy at MLK Aquatic & Recreation Center 2018

Students at the 411 Brand Basketball Academy at MLK Aquatic & Recreation Center 2018

Students at the 411 Brand Basketball Academy at MLK Aquatic & Recreation Center 2018

John Thomas & Chaka Zulu at the 411 Brand Appreciation Awards Ceremony at the Nike Store at Lenox in 2018

John Thomas & Big Tigger at the 411 Brand Appreciation Awards Ceremony at the Nike Store at Lenox in 2018

Chaka Zulu, Shanti Das, John Thomas, Big Tigger, Tamera Young and Chris Hicks at the 411 Brand Appreciation Awards Ceremony at the Nike Store at Lenox in 2018

John Thomas, Joy Young (middle) and the staff at Nike honoring a 411 Brand Student with a gift pack from the Jordan Brand in 2019

John Thomas returns to V103 Radio for the first time since he resigned in 1995 to speak with Greg Street about The 411 Brand in 2018.

FAILURE

5.

Failure

Failure n. fail·ure the condition or fact of not achieving the desired end or ends.

Some people treat Failure as a negative when in actuality, failure teaches you the most valuable life lessons. Failure shows you what you need to work on to become better. Failure tests your character as well. Anyone that achieved some type of success in life has also failed. It's those that did not give up after failing that usually becomes successful.

One day I called my guy Ash Cash, to ask him his thoughts on failure. Ash is one of the nations top personal financial experts and a best-selling author of over 10 books. I asked him how does he view failures? Is it something he tries to stay away from or accepts it as part of the journey to success? He said, "I think a lot of people would look at the word failure as the opposite of success. But for me, when I think of the word failure, failure is actually a part of success. During my journey, if it wasn't for all *of the failures that I had, I wouldn't have succeeded in a lot of things. So when I think of failure, I'm like, bring it on, the faster I fail, the more I'll know what not to do. So that way, I get closer to what actually needs to be done to maintain that level of success that I'm looking for." Today, Ash travels the world sharing his knowledge of how to attain financial freedom along with how to become a successful self- published author.*

After a series of great shows at Magic Johnson Theaters with some incredible guests, I was looking to begin to expand 411 to invite successful individuals outside of the music & sports industries. I had a relationship with someone who worked at Turner Broadcasting Network in Atlanta. She was explaining to me that Turner was the home to several networks outside of TNT & TBS. They also own the Cartoon Network, which had all of the great cartoons from the past along with some new programming. She invited me to Turner to meet some of the folks that made the network run and to see if there was any synergy. The staff was great and I met some cool folks and actually learned a lot in regards to how cartoons are actually made. We talked about what we were doing with 411 and we all thought it would be dope to invite some cool people from Cartoon Network on 411 to give students some insight on what really goes on behind their favorite cartoons. We were able to secure 4 great guests from the network to come and share their journey with over 250 students from three different Atlanta High Schools. There were two illustrators who actually created the cartoon Powder Puff Girls characters, an Executive Producer who developed the Powder Puff Girls cartoon for television and a writer, who wrote for 3 different cartoons on the network. I was excited. This was totally different for us and really showed that we really had the potential to grow and invite other industries to share their expertise and journey on our show.

As always, I worked closely with the staff at Magic Johnson Theaters to prepare for the program. There were a lot of moving parts but by this time we were vets at setting up everything from cameras, sound systems and having volunteers in place to help with the students and other detailed efforts. Chaka Zulu, Manager for Music & Film Star Ludacris and Co-Founder of Disturbing Tha Peace, was our host at the time. Chaka was never the guy to arrive early lol but would be there right on time. This day he shocked me when he pulled up early. Chaka was a self-described cartoon freak and was prepared! At this time, I really felt good about the moment we were about to have with Cartoon Network.

As we started to get closer to the start of the program, I realized that the school buses hadn't arrived yet. They normally arrive 30 to 45 minutes before the start of the program. I asked around to see if anyone had heard from the schools because we were getting close to start time. The answer was no and suddenly I felt my stomach drop. Everything is in place from staff, guests, hosts, cameras, audio, venue and everything else in between. But the least worry I had at the time was the students not arriving. I called my contact at Atlanta Public Schools to check on the ETA of the buses and express our readiness for the moment. Instantly, I heard it in her voice, "John, I am so sorry. I told the schools the wrong date of the program, they were prepared to come to the theater tomorrow."

Immediately, I felt like the world was over at that moment. I have all these people here at the theater early, ready to dedicate their time and energy to my vision and we will have nobody in the audience! I failed! How do I go in the room and tell all of these people that we will have no show today because the students will not be coming to the theater. I could blame Atlanta Public Schools, I could blame my contact or I could blame the schools individually but at the end of the day, it was my responsibility to confirm everything. No excuses. I went to Chaka and told him about the mix-up and he looked at me with a look that said, so what are we going to do? He asked if we could reschedule but with so many moving parts it would be difficult. So, I had to own it and look everyone in their eyes and tell them that we will not have a show today because of the scheduling mix-up. I could sense the disappointment when I told them but to my surprise they took the news very well. They all understood that it was out of my control and offered to reschedule at a later date if possible because they were really looking forward to the opportunity.

As my team packed up the equipment and said goodbye to our guests, I decided to stay back with the intention of being alone and drowning in my sorrows. Although everyone was really nice about it, I really felt like I let everyone down. I questioned myself, questioned the program and actually felt that could be a sign to move on from the program and put my energy into something else. Yes, I know this sounds a bit dramatic. But keep in mind, this was the first time that I experienced this type of disappointment where I invited everyone to an event that I was responsible for and had to cancel due to something I mishandled. I have always kept my disappointments to myself so that I could make sense of everything before getting the thoughts and opinions of others and this was one of those times.

In my disappointment, I decided to watch a movie by myself for the first time ever. I asked the manager of the theater which movie he would recommend. He suggested the movie Jerry McGuire, which just came out that week and he heard it was good. So, I got my popcorn and soda and sat in an empty theater (it was around 11am on a Wednesday) to watch the movie. To my surprise, the movie was excellent. It was exactly what I needed at that exact moment. The movie was extremely inspirational, motivational and spoke directly to me in regards to how to handle disappointment. If you haven't seen the movie it was about the relationship between an agent that was fired and a football player he represented that really believed in him as an agent and wouldn't leave him although all of his other clients did. The movie starred Tom Cruise and Cuba Gooding Jr.

On my drive home, I was reminded that things will happen in your life that appears not to be in your favor but was designed to strengthen your belief and prepare you for what is next. Failure is a mindset that you choose to believe and apply to your life. Instead of looking at your unsuccessful efforts as a failure, look at them as lessons that will help you and others along the journey moving forward

To help with dealing with Failure

- Remind yourself that you are not the first person to fail at something. Life isn't over.
- Accept your role in the failure & look for the lessons so that you don't repeat.
- Don't be afraid to share your failure with others. Others may have the answers you need..

Notes_____

_____

_____

_____

_____

_____

_____

_____

_____

_____

_____

_____

_____

_____

_____

_____

Notes_____

_____

_____

_____

_____

_____

_____

_____

_____

_____

_____

_____

_____

_____

_____

_____

_____

_____

HUMILITY

6.

Humility
Humble n. hum·ble marked by modesty in behavior, attitude, or spirit; not arrogant or prideful.

T here is a fine line between being confident and being cocky. Sometimes we tend to think that we're invincible or better than others because of a gift that God has given us. Instead of praising him for the gift, we brag to the world how good we are and that we're so special. Yes, we are special but only because God allowed us to be. When we fail at something, I believe it's humility that reminds us to tap back into our God and ask for his guidance.

"I reached out to my man Rob Lanier, whom I've known since we were 10/11 years old. I asked him his thoughts on humility and how did he deal with it in regards to his profession. He said "At a young age, I became a Head Coach at the Division 1 college level at 32, and had some mixed reviews. But, by the time I turned 36, I was fired. When you get fired as a Division 1 Head Coach, it's a public thing. It's on the ticker on the bottom of ESPN. As *well as if you're in a community where the program has some notoriety, it's a public failure. I experienced that, and I experienced the self- doubt and humility that comes from that. It was the first time that I had been a failure per se. So I learned some valuable lessons during that time." Rob has been a Division 1 Basketball Coach for over 35 years. He has coached at several of the top schools in the country including University of Texas, University of Florida and University of Virginia to name a few. He is currently the Head Coach at SMU University in Dallas, TX.*

While working at V103, 411 was really building a name for itself in Atlanta. We were going to different schools throughout the city inviting great guests discussing important topics and the show was hosted by V103 Radio Personality Carol Blackmon. I felt that we had all the necessary pieces to begin offering the program to the public. Up until this point, we held the program at locations that already had a built-in audience, like schools. So, I sat down with Carol and shared with her that I met the owner of a teen club in East Point called, "My Brother's Keeper" on Campbellton Road behind Greenbriar Mall. On one side of the building, it was a place that teens could go and hang with friends, dance and let their hair down. On the other side was large auditorium with a stage, lights, sound system and could seat 400-500 people. The owner heard about what we were doing throughout the school system and suggested that we do a collaboration of some kind since were serving the same audience. I liked the possibility of putting something together and felt that we could come up with something special.

So, I sat down with my boss, Joe Libios at V103 and told him about the conversation with the owner. We discussed that I wanted to produce an episode of the 411 Knowledge & Entertainment Show at My Brother's Keeper in front of a live audience. He was super supportive of this vision I had and gave his support from the station's promotion department. He suggested that I go speak with Tony Brown who was the station's Program Director to see if they could make space on the air for radio mentions and PSA's to support the event. I went down to Tony's office, explained the vision and he committed to helping to promote the event.

He said that I had to secure guests that were relevant to the station's audience so that it would make sense for their support. So, I met with Carol to discuss the run of show and who we should reach out to as guests. We decided to speak about the importance of HBCU's and invite some successful people that attended various HBCU's across the country. We invited comedian Jonathon Slocumb, music executive Lamont Boles and a student that committed to attend a HBCU that semester. We also had on the program as our musical guests, a group named Parental Advisory, from the Dungeon Family with my guy Kawon "KP" Prather. On paper everything looked great. We started promoting the event two weeks before the date.

The station really followed through on what they committed to and even went above and beyond. Carol and her co-host Mike Roberts even mentioned it on the Morning Show which has tremendous reach. As you can imagine, we're feeling great about the event and looking forward to growing the program outside of the school system.

I started to notice that we weren't getting a lot of kids signing up in advance but that wasn't unusual. We didn't require pre-registration because we felt that there were plenty of seats to accommodate everyone. So now it's the day of the event, everyone that was involved with pre-production arrived on time to set everything up. I kept walking back and forth to the door anticipating a crowd of people lined up to come in. There was no one there yet. I told myself we had time, it was still early. We had about 60 minutes before showtime. Our guests started to arrive. Parental Advisory was doing a brief sound check to make sure everything was working properly. We met with the other guests to discuss the run of show and they expressed how much they were looking forward to the program. Now we are 30 min before showtime and there are only 2 people in the audience. Yes, two PEOPLE! The venue held over 400 people and there were only two people there. Now I'm beginning to get this feeling that what if nobody shows up, what would I do? The clock seemed as if its starting to move faster than normal. We are now 15 min before showtime, then 10 min before, now 5 minutes before the start. My stomach is in knots because this was my idea. I asked everyone to participate and to dedicate their time to my vision and now what do I do?

We have been promoting this event for the past 2 weeks and there were only two people in the audience. My first thought was to cancel it and go home to lick my wombs. Carol came over to me and asked what were we going to do? I didn't have an answer. My pride wouldn't allow me to just confess to her that I didn't know what to do. I felt that if I asked everyone to participate and dedicate their time, I needed to figure it out. We are now 30 minutes beyond showtime and I'm starting to feel the antsy energy from everyone in the air. I kept walking to the door, calling people that committed to come out, anything that I could think of to not face the reality that I needed to make a decision soon. Lamont Boles, who was like a mentor to me, came up to me outside and directly asked me what was I going to do? I said, "I have to cancel the event. I really really felt bad that I wasted everyone's time". He could see the despair on my face and in my demeanor. He said "Why? You have everyone here, ready to go why cancel it?" "I said nobody showed up. This was an event created for a live audience. It's what we have always done."

He went on to explain to me that when television shows are made in LA, there's no audience. Some are done for the camera to be shown to an audience later. I immediately felt better because I had a lot of respect for Lamont. He approached me in a way to help solve the issue and not from a place of why I wasted his time, meant a lot. Although this was way before social media and YouTube, he talked about the importance of creating content. So, we walked back inside, I felt better but I still had to face everyone else. Amazingly, they all looked at me like I was bugging for even thinking about canceling it. We discussed that we were going to set up a camera and move forward with the show. To my surprise they were incredibly professional and went on with the show as if it was a packed house. There was great conversation between the guests, storytelling, laughter and I began to feel that this event really had a purpose. After the knowledge portion of the show came to an end, we're now preparing for the entertainment part of the program. Parental Advisory was to participate in a Q/A with Carol and then perform their new single afterwards. I went over to KP and said, you guys don't have to perform since we don't have an audience and I didn't want them to feel awkward. He said "Oh, we are definitely going to perform. It's what we do and what we love to do." Wow! I was ready to pull the plug on the event and to now see that everyone was ready to not only see it to the end but give 110% to make sure it was a success. Parental Advisory gave an incredible performance. They performed as if it was a packed house. Once their performance was over, everyone came over and thanked me for the opportunity. It really felt genuine and although I was still secretly beating myself up, their energy really helped my get out of my own way and begin to look at the positives of the day. I have always been very confident in everything that I put my mind and time into. But this day humbled me in a way that I had never faced before. I didn't have an answer to the issues that faced us that day. I had to confess to someone in that moment, I didn't know what to do. Fortunately, I had some great people around me whose energy showed me that despite there not being a live audience, everything else worked out perfectly. As we were about to leave, Lamont came over to me and asked, with there not being an audience, would I have done anything differently? My answer was no, I was extremely pleased with the outcome and grateful to everyone that contributed to the day. He told me directly, "the lesson of the day is that you control what you can control and whatever you can't let God handle it. If it works out in your favor, it was meant to be, if not, it was still meant to be but begin to search for the lesson and never forget it".

To help in dealing with Humilty

- Accept the fact that everything will not always go the way you planned it to go.
- Never be afraid to admit that you need help with something that you don't know
- Be willing to face adversity head on so that you can deal with it and move forward

Notes_____

_____

_____

_____

_____

_____

_____

_____

_____

_____

_____

_____

_____

_____

_____

_____

_____

_____

_____

Notes

GROWTH

7.

Growth
Growth n. growth development from a lower or simpler to a higher or more complex form.

Everyday we have an opportunity to grow and become a better person. This only happens when you allow yourself to face your fears and walk confidently in the life that God has allowed you to

live. Growth isn't just a bunch of good decisions that allows you to attain anything your heart desires. It's when things don't go your way and you still find it within you to be thankful for your life and everyone in it.

I was having a conversation with my guy Robert "Red" Rushin to get his thoughts about the importance of Growth and if he saw times in his life when he was stagnant and wasn't grow-ing. He said, "When I was in college, I felt that I was working hard, practicing and taking the game serious. But there wasn't any significant growth in my game. Once I finished college and *started training with NBA players, I started seeing the little things they did to get better. It was their consistency and how they challenged themselves to become better players. I realized at that moment why my game wasn't growing. I was just maintaining in college. I wasn't really pushing myself to the limit."*

He said, "Going through college, I knew I was better than a lot of the people I played against and having my sight on the NBA, I just thought what I was doing was enough. Now being around people that really do this, seeing their work ethic and seeing how hard they work, I quickly understood why my game didn't grow while in college." Red quickly figured it out though. He has several successful businesses including Weight No More, a full scale health and wellness organization designed for everyone interested in a healthy fit lifestyle owned by him and his fiancé Toya Wright in Atlanta.

As I look back over this journey, one of the major issues I had to wrestle with within myself was overthinking the process. I've always been a confident person but I realized that my confidence came from comfort. As most, when you have the knowledge, history and support of any new endeavor, you attack what's in front of you with excitement and vigor. You're making decisions on the fly, accepting any mistakes that may come and brush them to the side. You're confidently sharing any lack of knowledge about what you're doing with supportive people within your circle.

The 411 Brand was a one of one. It didn't exist before me. I convinced myself that there was nobody around me that knew how to navigate what I was dealing with on a daily basis in building this brand from scratch. So, most times I subscribed to the motto, "I'll figure it out."

I still deal with this mindset from time to time. But what I have learned is that nobody has all of the answers and collaboration is necessary in building a brand. There was a time back in 1996 when I partnered with Magic Johnson Theaters to host our 411 Knowledge & Entertainment Show Tour. This partnership allowed 411 to offer our program to students outside of the school setting. We were able to invite students from various schools, discuss topics that we felt were relevant without having to filter it because of the school's beliefs. We began receiving more attention throughout Atlanta for the work we were doing and as the program continued to grow rapidly, I quickly realized that I needed help. I was introduced to a young lady who was a Public Relations Manager at Turner. I shared with her my vision and expressed my desire to grow 411 to a level of impacting students all over Atlanta as well as across the country. She quickly understood my vision and agreed to come join our team and lend her expertise in public relations. She began to put together a plan of action that included me doing interviews, inviting press and tastemakers to attend our shows, as well as sharing thoughts on changing aspects of the show to make it better. Again, she worked for one of the leading cable networks in the world and really knew what she was talking about. As weeks went by, I started to feel like I was losing control over my own show, which was far from the truth.

Over the years, I have learned that insecurity plays a large role in your growth as an individual. Because you may not know how things may turn out with something that you're passionate about, we tend to second guess the outcome. Doubt creeps in and begins to cloud the original vision you felt so confident about. But you must continue to remain diligent in pursuing your goals despite being unsure of your next move. As I mentioned before, if you're the smartest person in the room then you're in the wrong room. In order to continue to grow as a person you must surround yourself with knowledgeable people that may know more about what you're doing than you. This can be intimidating but it also gives you the opportunity to become much more knowledgeable about what you're doing which can lead to the success you're looking for.

To help with dealing with Growth

- Never be afraid to challenge yourself by seeking knowledge from others.
- Set goals. There must be a plan of action that gets you closer to achieving your vision.
- Don't be afraid to fail. Failure teaches you lessons that are needed to succeed.

Notes

Notes_____

_____

_____

_____

_____

_____

_____

_____

_____

_____

_____

_____

_____

_____

_____

SUCCESS

8.

Success
Success n. suc·cess the achievement of something desired, planned, or attempted.

Success has many different definitions. As individuals, we must decide what success means to us. To me, success is being able to live your life on your own terms without compromising the gifts and talents God has given you to take care of your family and community. Success is always in the eyes of the beholder. But true success is when other lives are better because of your ability to work hard and tap into your purpose.

I reached out to my friend Darian "Big Tigger" Morgan and asked him his thoughts on Success and if achieving success in radio and TV was a main focus along his journey. He said, "It was and still is a main focus. This is my 28th year in radio, and 25th year in television. I would consider myself successful being that I've been here over a quarter century doing both of those things at a high level. But it's one thing to obtain success and another thing to remain in that success." he said.

I also asked him, how does he deal with being unsuccessful in something he's doing. How do you handle that part of your journey? "Most people would not know a bunch of the struggles that I've had to go through personally or career wise, because I keep it pushing. But there have been many times where I've fallen flat on my face, and had to pick myself up and keep going. But in any situation where success is fleeting, or is challenging or hard to obtain, you got to keep pushing. If it's something you really want and something you really want to do, it's a must that you keep working on it." Big Tigger has definitely pushed hard to achieve all of his goals in life. In addition to the incredible journey he has had in radio and television, he is currently the Morning Show Host on V103 Radio in Atlanta, the Atlanta Hawks Game Announcer, as well as the Team DJ for the Atlanta Falcons.

When I first started 411 back in 1992, money was the last thing on my mind. I didn't create this brand for a dollar. I created it as a way to create a place to connect the dots between successful individuals and young people striving for success. Also, I was unaware how to create a monetary value to our program.

Growing up, my goal was to get an athletic scholarship to a Division 1 College or University. When I was in about 6th or 7th grade, my parents, siblings and I were sitting around the table discussing college. We weren't poor by any stretch of the imagination but for my parents to come up with $100K for all five of us to attend college was definitely going to be tough. They drilled into us that in order to become successful in life we must attend college. So I remember telling my mother at 12 yrs old that they didn't have to worry about paying for me to attend college because I would get a full athletic scholarship after I graduate from High School. Although nobody has never received an athletic scholarship in my family, she calmly said, "Ok, I believe you!" That was it. That was the battery I needed in my back to go on a quest to achieve this goal.

Everything I did from that day forward was put through a filter of, "if I do X, will it help me to achieve my goal of going to a Division 1 College or University for free"? It was this mindset that held me accountable for my future success. Through my God-given talent, hard work and a little bit of luck, I was able to achieve my goal and receive a Division 1 Full Scholarship to Samford University. I graduated on time with a Journalism/ Mass Communication Degree and was able to walk across the stage with my mother smiling in the audience.

But this path to success didn't always translate as an entrepreneur in the business world. As an athletic recruiter, they will come to your games to watch you play to see if your talents would help their team. They will do their research and ask other coaches about you, but it will be up to them if your talents warrant receiving an athletic scholarship. In business, you have to learn how to articulate your vision clearly and consistently in order to have a chance to achieve success. This was a tough learning lesson for me. I always believed that if you're good at what you do, you will be noticed for your work and rewarded. But I quickly realized that no matter how good you are, if you don't share your vision, it would be difficult to achieve the goals you have set for yourself.

One day, in 1995, I woke up with excruciating stomach pain. I got out of bed but couldn't stand up straight. I then began to spit up blood. I was scared because I had no idea what was happening to me, so I called my mother. She told me to call the doctor immediately because it sounded like I had an ulcer. I was only 27 years old, extremely healthy and scared. I called my doctor and he asked that I come in immediately.

I went in and just like my mother said, I had a pretty bad peptic ulcer. He told me to take two weeks off from work and rest. Nothing else, only rest. The next day I went to meet with my then attorney Vernon Slaughter. Vernon was a very successful attorney in the music industry. He was a wise man. In addition to being my attorney, he was also my mentor. I went to him for help with many things that went on in my life in which I needed some type of guidance. I told him about the ulcer and what the doctor prescribed. He quickly told me that this moment would be a tremendous blessing in my life. I would be able to use this time to really assess my life up until this point and define what I wanted to do next. I was currently at

V103 Radio with an important, yet time consuming position. Although I worked my way up in the station to have an instrumental role, I was unhappy.

On the outside, it appeared as if I was living a young man's dream by working at the #1 radio station in the Southeast. But there was an external conflict between my role at the station and my passion for continuing to develop the 411 Brand. During my conversation with Vernon, he told me to take the next 14 days and only focus on the type of lifestyle that I wanted to live. He asked, "What was success to me? As you rest, live your life from a successful mindset. Don't focus on money because it doesn't equate to happiness." He went on to share stories of how many of his very wealthy clients, behind closed doors were extremely unhappy. They don't have meaningful relationships that they can turn to when they're in a time of need. Everything in their lives were predicated by the dollar. They lived in fear of losing everything, not realizing that what they were trying to protect had no value in things that their soul needed. He advised that I don't go down that road because it's lonely and he sees it daily in his office.

So as always, I took Vernon's advice and began to live my best life for two weeks. We had a pool and workout center in my apartment complex. Everyday, I scheduled my morning to consist of meetings about 411, great workout along with a 30-minute swim. After the workout, I would then shower and head down to Buckhead. I had a good friend named Mary Amado, who worked at Hotel Niko on Peachtree Rd. It was a luxury hotel that many of the music industry executives and artists stayed at while in Atlanta. She ran the restaurant in the hotel. I shared with her about my ulcer and the marching orders Vernon had given me. She gave me a stack of restaurant meal cards that were given to guests that stayed in the hotel for free breakfast or lunch. Everyday for two weeks, I would go to Hotel Niko to work and set up meetings centered around 411 at the hotel over breakfast or lunch.

Vernon was right. What you focus on consistently becomes a lifestyle. I started to feel that I was missing out on life by going to work everyday and focusing on anything other than what I was passionate about. I could really get use to this!

After my two weeks were up and I was fully healed from my ulcer, I returned back to V103. I was energized, focused and looking forward to figuring out how I could combine the new lifestyle that I was introduced to and the reality of having a job that requires you to work 50+ hours a week. Now don't get me wrong, I had a very cool job. At 24 years old, I was in a position that most would envy at that age. I had access to all the events in the city. (keep in mind that this was during the early to mid-90' swhen V103 was the only thing moving in regards to radio in Atlanta). So on paper, I was doing it. But after those two weeks, I realized that none of that matters if you are not spending the majority of your day doing what you're passionate about.

I returned to work on a Monday. As I walked into my office, I instantly noticed that in addition to the work that I left on my desk two weeks ago, the pile had doubled! I instantly felt a sharp pain in my stomach. My doctor told me that an ulcer is your body's way of reacting to stress. I realized that I had a habit of internalizing anything that was bothering me and then try to figure out how to deal with the situation. By internalizing the situation, I was creating an enormous amount of stress on my body and it showed itself in various forms, with one being the ulcer.

On Thursday of that week, I met with my boss Joe Libios and explained to him how I was feeling about my job, the pain in my stomach when I returned back to work and was considering resigning from my position at the station. If you every met Joe, he was a short guy that was extremely persistent and had the ability to promote anything. He epitomizes the Jay Z lyric, "I can sell water to a whale!" He offered several solutions and asked is there anything that he could do that would get me to stay at the station? He also told me that there was a new hip-hop station coming to Atlanta called Hot 97.5. The station's format was going to specifically target young people who loved hip-hop. He said that the station will be on air in about a month or so and he could get me in as the Promotions Director easily, especially with my experience coming from V103.

This was an interesting opportunity to be part of the genesis of a new radio station in Atlanta where the music played was exactly what I listened to everyday. I told him that I would consider it and lets talk tomorrow. I went home and called my mother to explain to her the position that I was in and to see if she could help me make the best decision. She really focused on my health and brought up if I was having these issues at V103, the #1 station in the Southeast what would it look like working at a start up hip-hop station competing for a part of V103's listeners? After some thought, I realized accepting this opportunity would be like jumping out of the pot into the frying pan. Radio promotion is a 24-hour, 7 day a week job. It requires an immense amount of passion to be successful in radio promotions. That's one thing I admired about Joe, he really loved the art of promotions. Although it was an incredible opportunity to be part of Atlanta Radio History as the Promotions Director at Atlanta's first hip-hop station, I had to be honest with myself.

On Friday, the last day of the first week since I returned to work, I walked into V103/WAOK General Manager Rick Mack's office and handed him my resignation letter. He asked my why and I told him about my ulcer experience and that I was no longer passionate in my position. He seemed interested in my reasoning and outlook on the decision. He shared a similar situation that happened along his journey, wished me luck and offered to help in any way that he could, in which I really believed his sincerity. I walked out his office with my head up high. I was making a life-altering decision by choosing to follow my spirit and walk directly into the unknown. I had a vision, wrote it out, put my blinders on and Got Busy!

To help Achieve your Success

- When creating your success, make sure it's in direct alignment with your soul.
- Don't be afraid to take risks along your journey.
- Surround yourself with people that know more than you and has your best interest.

Notes_____

_____

_____

_____

_____

_____

_____

_____

_____

_____

_____

_____

_____

_____

_____

_____

_____

Notes_____

_____

_____

_____

_____

_____

_____

_____

_____

_____

_____

_____

_____

_____

_____

_____

_____

_____

EPILOGUE

Wow! As I look back on an incredible 30-year journey, I view the creation and the development of the 411 Brand as one of my greatest accomplishments in my lifetime. Being able to see a potential void in youth development and execute a plan of action that would impact tens of thousands of young people during this 30-year period, has been amazing. Then to develop and attach a monetary value for the offering that has accumulated hundreds of thousands of dollars over this 30-year period has been equally amazing.

When I first started 411, I knew it would be a valuable resource for parents and kids across the country. But how does that happen? If you do not have access to someone that has actually done the leg work and can give you a play by play of how to achieve success in this space, you will have to start from scratch. The kids say "get it from the mud." There have been many times that I wished someone came in, saw the vision and stepped in to assist financially, as well as with their expertise in business development. That never happened.

Don't get me wrong, I have received a tremendous amount of support over the years. But I have never received the "Come here young fella, let me walk you through this process." To be honest, I never placed myself in the position of needing help for that to happen, so with that I own my shortcomings wholeheartedly. It's always been important to me to call my own shots or at least have a hand in any decisions concerning my livelihood.

The 411 Brand has grown into a successful youth development organization in Atlanta that offers educational, entertainment and athletic programs to young people across the country. With various partnerships including the City of Atlanta, Atlanta Police Foundation, My After School Program and several others, we are currently providing quality after school programming to close to a thousand young people a year throughout Metro Atlanta. We are looking for that number to double if not triple in 2023, as we introduce our **411 Brand Saturday School Program** in Atlanta and eventually throughout the country.

The 411 Brand Saturday School Program is designed to give young people a safe, recreational, fun, productive space during non-school hours where they can engage in quality programming that will provide non-traditional learning opportunities. Students enrolled in the 411 Brand Saturday School will be given an opportunity to select programs that they're passionate about in an effort to have a major impact in their growth and development. 411 Brand will offer programs that are designed to teach the fundamentals of each offering, as well as provide the necessary knowledge to transfer these skills to prepare for possible employment opportunities.

One of the challenges that we have faced over the years was how to create a culture surrounding our programs without our own space. We have been providing programming in our partner's facilities throughout the years because it has been a win-win for everyone involved. But it has been difficult to create a certain type of culture in someone else's house when you're only there for 2-3 hours a week. In an effort to develop the culture we feel is necessary and that will be consistent with programming, we are currently taking steps to build the first 411 Brand Education & Athletic Center in Atlanta.

The 411 Brand Education & Athletic Academy Center is a full-circle facility designed to create a multi-platform environment that provides programming to enlighten young people in the areas of entertainment, education & athletics. We provide effective, safe and transparent programming for students between the ages of 6-21. Our staff consists of diverse experts to support young people seeking to reach their full potential. Mentorship is huge with us! This location will also be a home for mentors to come in and share their journey, as well as the knowledge they acquired along the way with young people. We're building a culture where a student that's enrolled in the music academy will have access to a plethora of music artists, producers, songwriters, lawyers etc., who are willing to speak into the next generations of artists. Students enrolled in business and marketing will have an opportunity to share the same space with successful entrepreneurs and marketing gurus, willing to share their knowledge and expertise with the students. This facility will change the way youth development programming will impact the young people moving forward.

When I was around 24 or 25 years old, there was a Life Coach Specialist that came into the offices at V103 to speak with our department about how to maximize your time everyday. He said one of the keys to life was to make time to step out of your day-to-day life to assess everything that you have going on and develop a daily plan of action to get closer to your goals. He shared an important and life-altering thought process that I have carried with me from that day forward. He shared the concept of, "Have, Do, Be", which was the very first time that I heard of this concept.

The "Have, Do, Be mindset has been taught to us unconsciously by are parents, guardians, family and those that we looked up to growing up. Most of us think we need to "have" a certain thing or set of things (more money, love, time, experience, etc.), so that we can finally "do" something important (pursue our passion, start a business, go on vacation, create a relation-ship, buy a home, etc.), which will then allow us to "be" what we truly want in life (peaceful, fulfilled, inspired, generous, in love, etc.). In actuality, it works the other way around. First, we "be" what we want (peaceful, loving, inspired, abundant, successful, or whatever), then we start "doing" things from this state of being – and soon we discover that what we're doing ends up bringing us the things we've always wanted to "have." This is an introverted mindset that forces you to look inside to discover who you fully are and then share that with the world. Unfortunately, especially with young people, we tend to look out into the world to discover who we are or want to be and sometimes that doesn't match up with who we're destined to be in the world.

We all have 24-hours in a day to to live our best life. If we break down the day, you will be able to see where you can make adjustments that would bring you closer to managing the time you have to achieve your goals. For example, if we sleep for 8 hours, work for 8 hours there is only 8 hours left in the day. If you travel back and forth to work and live in a major city, let's say thats 2 ½ hours in traffic on the low end. Now we're at 5 ½ hours left in the day.

If you're into living a healthy lifestyle and staying in shape, you will spend at least an hour in the gym or exercising. Now, we're at 4 ½ hours left in the day. If you're blessed to have a family or looking forward to having one, as sad as this sounds, lets give your family (your spouse and children) 3 hours a day of your time. Now you have 90-min left in the day for errands, friends, meditation, social media, extended family, your community, events, as well as other things that are important in your life. Unfortunately, this is the schedule of over 80% of adults in our society. We have to make a conscious effort to create the life we want to live because if you don't, life will pass you by and you would be left with a bunch of should've, could've, would've's moments. Take control of your life and make choices that allow you every chance to be successful. Remember, success is personal. You choose what success looks like for you. Take ownership of the decisions that you make along the way. You're not a victim.

Every day that you wake up, you have a choice to either own every aspect of your life or look for excuses, as to why things don't go your way. Choose to own your life and take pride in knowing that life is a Journey and not a Destination.

So Buckle up and Enjoy the ride.

Made in the USA
Columbia, SC
21 April 2022

59301114R00075